LESSONS IN LEADERSHIP

A course for students in Years 6–12

PHIL RIDDEN

Edwest Publishing

Published by Edwest Publishing
Joondalup, Western Australia
www.edwestpublishing.biz

ISBN Paperback: 978-0-6489151-8-8
ISBN Ebook: 978-0-6489151-7-1

Contact Phil@philridden.biz

Cover image courtesy of Linus Nylund on Unsplash

TABLE OF CONTENTS

INTRODUCTION

Leadership is an important activity. It is critical that today's youth learn to understand and exercise leadership, not as a power to be lorded over others, but as a relational skill which can enrich their lives and the lives of others, and can facilitate great achievements.

Many people assume that leadership is a gift, which some have and others don't. While there is no doubt that some children, from an early age, exercise leadership and are looked upon as leaders by their peers, many students can learn to better use the leadership qualities which they have. In addition, students can be taught to recognise leadership qualities in others, qualities which go beyond bossiness and charisma.

This book is based on the author's experience in teaching leadership to students. It can be used with Primary and Secondary students, and can be adapted by the teacher to the needs of the group.

HOW TO USE THESE LESSONS

This program can be used across a range of ages, typically from Years 6 to 12, and has been designed to fit a series of 10 x 45 minute lessons. However, we honour the wisdom of teachers in adapting a program to their needs. For example:

- You might adjust the number or length of lessons to fit your timetable and your students.
- You might use the course at a camp, perhaps spread over two or more days.
- You may have ideas for changing some lessons to suit your teaching style or your students' particular needs.

Typically, schools provide leadership training for those students who are selected as leaders. We believe that *all* students should receive training in leadership because leadership is not for the select few, but for all (see Assumptions About Leadership), and because the understandings and attitudes taught in this program are valuable for everyone.

THE AUTHOR

Dr Phil Ridden has been a teacher of primary and secondary students, curriculum writer and consultant, professional development consultant, principal, executive and non-executive director of school boards, author and conference speaker — and parent.

Through writing, teaching and mentoring, he has shared with students and colleagues his extensive experience in leadership. He has been honoured by professional associations for his contribution to the professional growth of colleagues.

In this book, Phil shares some ideas for teaching students about leadership, in the knowledge that moral leaders make significant contributions to the welfare of others.

Contact him at www.philridden.biz

ASSUMPTIONS ABOUT LEADERSHIP

If we are to teach students about leadership, we must consider our own assumptions about leadership, because our assumptions influence the conscious and unconscious messages we give students.

Look at the views expressed in the chart below. To what degree do you agree with each statement? Can you cite examples to support your opinion?

Leaders are born.	Leadership is a social or relational skill (or a set of such skills) which can be learned.
	All students have the potential to lead. Reflective and focused experience of leadership can develop leadership insights and abilities.
Leadership capabilities are allocated to an elite few.	Any person with the desire to lead, a degree of commitment and purpose demanded by the situation can acquire and exercise successful leadership behaviour.
The leader of a group is visible by their assertive actions. They lead from the front.	The most influential leader of a group is not always obvious. They lead from the centre.
If a student does not display natural leadership, they will never be a leader. They don't have the skills or the presence.	If a student does not display natural leadership, it may be because: • they lack the confidence • they don't see the need • the school/classroom ethos discourages such action • their leadership skills lie in areas not usually relevant to classroom leadership.
Leaders are always leaders in any situation.	Different people show leadership in different situations. A leader in one situation may display leadership in another. Everyone can be a leader in some situation. Effective groups share leadership and allow different members to lead at different times.
Leaders are people of action.	Leaders are reflective.

Leadership is defined by a series of skills or abilities.	Leadership is a process of thinking and relating. It is seen as an interplay of complex interactions between a leader, other people involved and the situation.
Leaders are confident, devoid of doubt, and confident risk-takers.	Leaders are self-reflective. They often doubt their own abilities and judgements, and even their right to lead.
Leaders know exactly where they are going and what they must do.	Leadership is found in the place of not knowing, of change, of new learning, of new directions.
A leader's role is to get people to do as the leader wants in order to get the job done.	Leaders impact the way people behave and the way a group or organisation functions. They are intentionally inspirational, helping others to find their voice and purpose.

The understandings in the left-hand column are typical assumptions about leadership. They may not necessarily be wrong, but they are probably inadequate. This book is based on the understandings in the right-hand column. While some people are more naturally disposed towards leadership because of their personal and interpersonal qualities, others can learn to exercise leadership.

Sections of this course were conducted at a camp. After a series of practical activities, one student observed that leaders had emerged who were not seen as leaders in the classroom. It reminds us that contexts, opportunities, expectations and training all influence the practice of leadership.

CONCEPT 1. THE RIGHT ATTITUDE — PERHAPS I COULD DO THAT!

The purpose of this section is to create in each individual the awareness that they are not ordained to be or not be a leader, nor to lead in only one particular field (e.g. sport). Anyone can lead, given the right circumstances, motivation and confidence.

Understanding: By the end of the section, students may begin to think, 'He/She can lead. Why can't I?' They may have discovered 'Others think I'm a leader. Why don't I?'

Leadership attitude: When faced with a situation in which a leader is needed, I will think, 'PERHAPS I COULD DO THAT!'

LESSON 1A: MY PERSONAL KNOWLEDGE ABOUT LEADERS AND LEADERSHIP

Time required: Approximately 20 minutes

Outcomes

- We already have some knowledge about leadership.

- We can acquire more knowledge about leadership which can help us to become better leaders.

Learning experience

Ask students to prepare a personal concept map (or other summary format) about Leaders and Leadership. This may include names of leaders, qualities of leaders, what leaders do, leaders at school, how leaders become leaders, and so on. Then encourage them to add to the map their own questions about Leaders and Leadership. A template is offered as *Lesson 1A worksheet: About leadership.*

Context

There are four purposes for the concept map:

- To find out what students already know or believe about leadership.

- To serve as a baseline to evaluate changes in students' learning. The sheets could be photocopied and the copies kept until the end of the course and compared with each student's final map.

- To encourage students to reflect on their learning.

- To help students to map their own learning. As the course proceeds, students should add to their maps any new understandings or insights.

Throughout the course, commence each lesson with concept maps open, and add to it as new insights occur or questions arise.

Our experience

The students' maps showed us that they understood a great deal about leadership. Many responses showed that students saw leaders as responsible, skilled or talented, good listeners, helpful, organised, good examples, honest, decision makers, friendly …

Some also identified specific people whom they saw as leaders.

LESSON 1B: A SURVEY OF LEADERS IN THE CLASS

Time required: Approximately 25 minutes

Outcomes

- Some people are readily identifiable as leaders.

- People differ in their assessments of leaders.

- Various people may be seen as leaders depending on the situation — including some not normally thought of as leaders in the group.

Learning experience

Explain that you are going to name some situations in which a leader might be needed. The students are to think who in the class they would choose as a leader in each situation. They should write their answers privately, without discussion, and be confident to make their own choices. They may choose a peer for more than one category. Emphasise that this is not a popularity contest.

From your class (or year level) who would you choose to lead:

- A class sports team?

- A Science group?

- A project to make a class newspaper?

- The planning of your class assembly?

- The class (a class captain or prefect)?

Invite students to share responses with a partner, giving reasons for their choices. Then, in a whole class discussion, sample the responses from the class to each position, and draw general insights.

Context

Clearly, some level of trust is needed in the group for this discussion. Some students will be mentioned by name, with their positive qualities highlighted. Some will find this very affirming; others may be disappointed at not being selected. It may be necessary to discuss this before sharing insights, to emphasise that:

- Everyone's opinion is respected.

- It is not a popularity vote.

- It is not a declaration of friendship or animosity.

- The discussion does not have repercussions outside the classroom.

- The focus is not so much on who the leaders are, but on the particular qualities identified as necessary for each position.

This lesson is important in encouraging students to think about the qualities which make a leader, rather than on who the most obvious class leaders are.

Our experience

Typically, most students choose a skilled sportsperson to lead a sporting team, and a person with sound knowledge of Science to lead the Science group. However, it is interesting to explore those qualities cited by those who do not think a sports captain has to be the best in the team. They tended to choose as leader for the class newspaper someone with literary skills plus skills in organisation and communication, with the latter skills seen as important to lead the planning of a class assembly. The class captain is often seen as requiring personal qualities, such as fairness and honesty, rather than particular skills. The list of roles, therefore, implies a transition from specific skills to more generic skills and qualities.

However, usually a number of 'surprises' are identified, with students named who would not normally be listed as class leaders, yet with qualities which were clearly articulated. This is insightful on the part of the nominator, illuminating for the class and greatly affirming to the nominees.

Lesson 1A worksheet: ABOUT LEADERSHIP

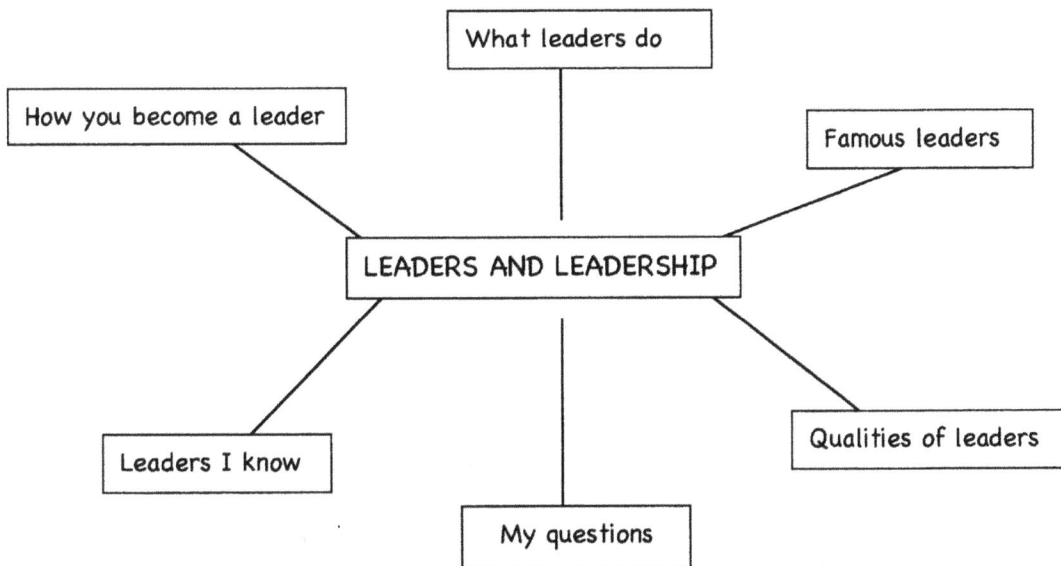

What leaders do

How you become a leader

Famous leaders

LEADERS AND LEADERSHIP

Qualities of leaders

Leaders I know

My questions

CONCEPT 2. THE RIGHT GOAL — TOGETHER, WE CAN MAKE A DIFFERENCE!

The purpose of this section is to create in each individual an understanding that, distilled to its essence, leadership is influence. Therefore, if we are to lead others, then who we are matters as much as what we do. Leaders lead with character. Their goal is to make a difference.

Understanding: By the end of the section, students may be considering, 'Who am I as a leader? How can I influence others?'

Leadership attitude: As a leader, I can influence others, even inspire them, so that they think, 'TOGETHER, WE CAN MAKE A DIFFERENCE!'

LESSON 2: ATTRIBUTES OF LEADERS

Time required: Home task — 1 week;
then as much time as possible in class, perhaps 2 x 45 minutes.

Outcomes

- There are many people – past and present, known through the media or known personally – who are leaders.

- There are identifiable qualities which mark these people as leaders.

- The key leadership qualities of leaders vary with the nature of the role; eg. A military leader may exhibit different qualities from a community leader.

Learning experiences

Students undertake a research task to gain and share insights about leadership. The task is described on *Lesson 2 worksheet: Attributes of leaders — research task.* (You may choose to use the word *attributes* or *qualities* or *traits* or *characteristics…*)

Students should be encouraged to discuss the task with family and friends, rather than to make it simply an intellectual research activity. Allow them to decide what to include and how to present it, encouraging creative approaches. The purpose is not to present a biography, but insights into leadership, so students may need to be reminded that their subject's date of birth, how they died, where they lived, what their parent's names were, and their liking for chocolate should not detract from those parts of the story which highlight their leadership qualities.

When complete, ensure that every student has the opportunity to present their work, orally or by display, as appropriate. While some students might present their work to groups peers, rather than the whole class, identify some, which are particularly insightful, for presentation to the whole class. This may require more than one lesson, if the time is available.

The essential outcome is that it provides for the class some understandings or insights into leadership.

(You might even like to ask students to consider why we chose the cover design for this book.)

Our experience

Students chose an amazing array of contemporary and historical leaders, sports people, local community leaders (including teachers and coaches) and even family members. Students identified a very perceptive list of leadership qualities, such as ability to innovate, perseverance, conviction and commitment, care for others, ability to make decisions, etc.

Interesting insights may emerge from discussions about people such as Hitler, who had ability to influence others, but was clearly not a moral leader.

Lesson 2 worksheet: ATTRIBUTES OF LEADERS — RESEARCH TASK

Homework research task. LEADERS AND LEADERSHIP.

Due:

Choose someone you think of as a leader. (They can be living or dead, but must be a real person.) Prepare a presentation about them which gives us some insights into leadership.

You may decide what to include in your presentation, but it must teach us something about leaders and leadership.

You may decide how to present it - writing, speaking, photos, drama, video, song, etc.

You may talk about this with your family, who can help you in any way they like — except for the final presentation!

Teacher:

Homework research task. LEADERS AND LEADERSHIP.

Due:

Choose someone you think of as a leader. (They can be living or dead, but must be a real person.) Prepare a presentation about them which gives us some insights into leadership.

You may decide what to include in your presentation, but it must teach us something about leaders and leadership.

You may decide how to present it - writing, speaking, photos, drama, video, song, etc.

You may talk about this with your family, who can help you in any way they like — except for the final presentation!

Teacher:

Homework research task. LEADERS AND LEADERSHIP.

Due:

Choose someone you think of as a leader. (They can be living or dead, but must be a real person.) Prepare a presentation about them which gives us some insights into leadership.

You may decide what to include in your presentation, but it must teach us something about leaders and leadership.

You may decide how to present it - writing, speaking, photos, drama, video, song, etc.

You may talk about this with your family, who can help you in any way they like — except for the final presentation!

Teacher:

Photocopiable page. Phil Ridden, *Lessons in Leadership,* www.philridden.biz, 2020

15

LESSON 3A and 3B: EXPERIENCING LEADERSHIP: A PRACTICAL TASK

Time required: Approximately 45 minutes each lesson

Outcomes

- Leaders are often important to the functioning of a group.

- Leaders are not necessarily the most dominant members of a group.

- Leaders play a variety of roles.

- Leaders can be identified as leaders because of what they do.

Learning experiences

Students undertake a group practical task. (See ideas below.) In 3A, the task is a classroom task; in 3B it is an outdoor task. Both activities are not essential, but the different challenges of an outdoor task may bring out different leaders from the classroom task. Note that:

- The groups are intentionally quite large, perhaps 8 or so.

- The groups are structured randomly, or in such a way that there is a variety of personalities in each group, ideally bringing together students who might not normally choose to work together.

- Group leaders are *not* appointed.

- The task can be complicated in various ways to magnify the difficulties with group dynamics and to provide opportunity for different leaders to emerge.

After the activity, discuss questions such as these:

- Who was the leader in your group initially?

- How did they get to be leader?

- Why did the group accept them as the leader?

- What did they do to help the group to achieve the goal?

- How did they handle the group dynamics – the uncooperative, the argumentative, the would-be leader, the independents, etc?

- Did the leadership change hands? Why?

- Did other people exercise leadership? What did they do?

If the process is complicated as suggested below, other questions will arise, such as:

- Were new members accepted by the group? Did they take time to find out what the group was doing? How did they find out? Did the new members try to change the group's ideas? How?

- How did the group respond to pressure (of shortened time, for example)? Did they become more focussed or less? Did a decisive leader emerge? Did the group more readily accept someone's leadership because of the 'crisis'?

Context

For the purposes of this course, the task itself is irrelevant. A task could be chosen which links to another area of the curriculum. The purpose is simply to give the group a task which will require them to work together, and will, ideally, put them under some pressure to complete the task successfully.

For LESSON 3A, use a classroom task.

For LESSON 3B, complete the task outdoors (it could be a camp activity, for example) and choose a task of a type not usually encountered in the classroom.

The groups are intentionally larger than might normally be considered appropriate for the task. The larger group puts stress on the working efficiency of the group, and enables the issues of teamwork, relationships and leadership to be magnified and better observed.

Some groups will work as a cluster of individuals; some will divide into independently functioning (even competing) subgroups; some will work together without any obvious coordination; some will have visible leaders; the leadership may change during the activity; different roles may be evident in some groups (ideas person, coordinator, implementer, questioner, etc.)

The introduction of complicating factors may magnify issues involved in group work. This may be particularly useful for groups which exhibit great harmony and cohesion, or those which seem unable to work together.

Notes

The task:

For the purposes of this course, the task itself is irrelevant. A task could be chosen which links to another area of the curriculum. The purpose is simply to give the group a task which will require them to work together, and will, ideally, put them under some pressure to complete the task successfully.

The task can be made simple or complex, according to the age and abilities of the students; for example:

Build a structure with these specifications:

- It must be built only of small (centimetre cube) blocks
- No joiners or adhesives may be used
- It must be free-standing
- It must stand as high as possible.

OR

- It must be built of newspaper and tape only.
- It must measure a minimum of 1.8 m at the tallest point
- It must be self supporting and movable
- Its interior must accommodate at least one group member.

OR

Ropes courses, obstacle courses, and adventure trails provide ideal contexts for outdoor problem solving tasks.

The complicating factors:

The task can be further complicated in ways such as these, depending upon the age and ability of the group and the particular requirements of the task. However, it is important that these factors do not destroy the credibility of the task or the commitment of each group to it.

- After about 10 minutes, choose a significant contributor in each group and move them to another group.

- After a reasonable time, announce that the time has been shortened and there are only three minutes left. At the same time announce that a prize will be offered to the highest tower.

- Announce a 5 minute strike of all female workers to protest wage inequities.

- Announce a 5 minute freeze on sitting or kneeling on the floor, due to suspected contamination of the floor.

- Ask each group to select 2 workers to move to another group for personal development.

- Merge pairs of groups.

Our experience

The discussion enabled students to begin to see that

- The bossiest person is not necessarily the leader.

- A quietly spoken person might exercise great influence on the group because of the value of their contributions, or because of their ability to coordinate members' efforts, or because of their ability to gain members' trust, etc.

- One quality of leadership is the ability to listen and to link members' ideas.

- The imposition of an assertive outsider into the group forces the group to consider whether the new ideas this person brings are useful to the group purpose or not.

- The sudden shortening of the time sometimes panics groups, which may cause leadership to be focused, or discarded.

Students were surprised to see that the outdoor activity allowed leaders to emerge who did not normally exhibit leadership within the classroom.

LESSON 4: OBSERVING LEADERSHIP

Time required: Approximately 45 minutes

This lesson is similar in its purpose to Lesson 3. However, the task is unlikely to succeed if everyone goes about it in their own way. Coordination of action is essential. This requires someone willing and able to lead and a group willing to allow them to lead.

The additional factor is that most of the students do not participate in the activity, but observe. The value in this activity is that it may:

- Enable some students to see in others what they may have been unable to see in their own group behaviour;

- Allow observers to recognise leadership which is not assertive, yet is still influential.

Learning experience

Provide each student with *Lesson 4 worksheet: Observing leadership.* Seat them around the activity area, and ask them to make and record observations about the group doing the activity. Observers may not make comments. Following the activity, invite the observers to provide feedback to the activity group and to ask why they reacted in particular ways.

Select a group of 8 or more students, containing a range of personalities and skills, and bringing together students who might not choose to work together. A leader is not normally appointed, unless you wish to challenge a particular student to lead.

Spread out a blanket or tarpaulin on the floor. The group must stand on it, so that no appendages are touching the ground off the blanket. If the group completes the stand, have them get off and fold blanket in half. Repeat the above process for as long as possible.

A variation you may prefer is to ask the group to turn the blanket completely over while still standing on it, with no-one touching the ground off the carpet.

(A task could be chosen which links to another area of the curriculum. The purpose is to give the group a task which will require them to work together, and will allow leaders to emerge.)

Our experience

It is an informative experience for students to observe another group's struggles, not just with the task, but with listening to the ideas of others, and allowing someone to take a lead. Some observers will feel a strong urge to intervene and tell them what to do, or who to listen to.

Lesson 4 worksheet: OBSERVING LEADERSHIP

Watch and listen to the group doing the activity. Make notes to help you to give feedback to the group later.

1. Who is the leader?

2. How did they get to be leader?

3. Why does the group accept them as leader?

4. What do they do to help the group achieve the goal?

5. How do they handle the group dynamics – people who don't want to help, who want to argue, who want to be leader, who want to do things differently from the rest of the group, etc.?

6. Does the leadership change hands? Why?

7. Do other people exercise leadership? What do they do?

Photocopiable page. Phil Ridden, *Lessons in Leadership,* www.philridden.biz, 2020

20

LESSON 5: WHERE DO LEADERS GET THEIR RIGHT TO LEAD?

Approximate time: 45 minutes

Outcomes

- Some leaders are given the authority to lead.

- Influence is most authentic source of power for leaders.

- Leaders do not need a title or appointed role to lead.

Learning experience

Ask students to bring media reports of incidents in which someone showed leadership. Examples might include a world leader making a speech, a sportsperson turning the tide of a game, a 'hero' rescuing someone from danger … If students bring a printout or clipping of articles, the story will be clearer and the reports can form a display.

Invite students to share in pairs or triads. Then ask them to explain to their partner what authority the person had to exercise leadership.

Ask students who influences them. Then explore how they influence them. Explain various sources of influence (see Context below) which leaders use. As each is discussed, invite students to share an example in triads or with the whole class.

Then explain to students the following sources of influence which people draw on when they exercise leadership.

Context

There are various ways to categorise forms of influence; e.g.:

- Positional authority: These people have the backing of an employing authority or other legal or regulatory source. However, positional authority is influential only as along as the people in these positions earn respect through their actions. Their positions merely buy them time to establish this.

- Expertise: This is derived from qualifications, experience or acquired knowledge. However,

    o the 'expert' may lose influence if they are arrogant or excessively critical of others; and

    o some online 'influencers' are ascribed expertise or credibility because their blog is popular or they have a high media profile, not because they have any actual expertise in an issue.

- Charisma: These people are given leadership status because they have attractive personalities and communicate in ways which connect with people, evoking an emotional response. Such people inspire and motivate us to do things we might normally be inhibited about.

- Role modelling: The attitudes and actions of 'heroes' influence people to emulate them.

- Reward and punishment: People tend to repeat actions which are rewarded, and avoid those which are punished. Coercion and manipulation are extensions of this.

- Appeal to motivation: People ask 'Can I do what is required? (ability) and 'Will it be worth it?' (motivation).

- Appeal to the heart: Some people appeal to people's emotions through their story or their example, inspiring others to join them.

Leaders use their influence in various ways:

- Influence can be used for 'good' or 'bad' purposes. In addition to being inspired to help others, we can be influenced by a leader to behave in an anti-social or criminal manner.

- Leaders may lead from the front, behind or centre; they may be highly visible or almost invisible; they may direct the group's actions (dictatorial or 'bossy'), help the group to choose its own way (democratic), or allow the group to find its own way (laissez-faire).

How do we respond to a leader's influence? Skilled leaders appeal to the heart. When they capture the heart, they capture the head and the hands as well. Often, we do not care who leads, as long as the leader inspires and motivates us, by appealing to our emotions and aspirations. Children and youth are particularly susceptible to such influence.

Our experience

Students are sometimes quite shocked to see how easily they are influenced by what their peers, their parents, or their sporting or entertainment heroes say and do. There are many examples in the media of this.

CONCEPT 3. THE RIGHT MOTIVATION — I'M HERE TO HELP!

The purpose of this section is to create in each individual an understanding that leaders are team players, concerned for the well-being and growth of others. They serve others.

Understanding: By the end of the section, students may be considering, 'Do I let others lead? How do I help others to feel good about themselves and their work? How can I affirm others?'

Leadership attitude: As a leader, I serve others, always thinking, 'HOW COULD I HELP YOU?' and assisting them to think, 'I COULD DO THAT!'

LESSON 6: GROUP ROLES AND LEADERSHIP

Time required: Approximately 45 minutes

Outcomes

- People in groups play different roles.

- The roles they play are related to their personalities and styles.

- Each role is important to the group, although particular groups in particular contexts might value the roles differently.

- People are more engaged if they feel they have a role and that that role is valued

- A high performing team has each role represented.

- Each member may lead at some time, depending on the need of the group at that time. There is synergy in using all the skills of the group members and in allowing others to lead.

Learning experiences

Choose a group of 8-10 students and set a creative task, which requires a fair amount of interaction and talking; e.g., create a card game or board game to teach about leadership. (As before, you may have a task which supports another area of the curriculum.)

Appoint the remainder of the class as observers, and equip them with *Lesson 6 worksheet: Group roles — observation sheet*.

The activity could involve more people by substituting 2 or 3 members of the groups with others during the activity.

Identify who played each of the roles on the sheet (see Context below).

Make it clear that no role is more important than another, although a particular role might be important at a particular stage of the task; e.g. at the commencement, the Plant (ideas person) might suggest ways to go about the task; when the work gathers momentum, the Co-ordinator might be needed to coordinate activity; if there is conflict the Team Worker may be needed to achieve harmony; etc.

Then invite students to talk with peers to identify what their natural role might be.

Context

This classification of roles is adapted from the work of Belbin (https://www.belbin.com/about/belbin-team-roles/). The descriptors on the Observation Sheet loosely define the roles in a way children can apply, identified by the following initials:

    CO = Coordinator
    SH = Shaper
    PL = Plant (Innovator)
    RI = Resource Investigator,
    ME = Monitor–Evaluator,
    IMP = Implementer
    TW = Team Worker,
    CF = Completer–Finisher.

Belbin also included the role of Specialist, who brings specialist knowledge to a given task.

An adapted version of the Team Roles, and a simple online test, can be found at www.123.com.

Within groups, no role is inherently more important than another. Well-structured groups have all roles represented.

Clearly, students do not need to learn these roles. A mature group of students might even define their own list of roles which they observe. The point of this activity is to help students to understand:

- that a group can have several leaders, who each leads in particular ways at particular times.

- that effective groups encourage people to lead, using their natural gifts, when the situation calls for those gifts;

- that while each of us has an inherent 'natural' role, in skilled groups members step into particular roles as needed, including those which are not their 'natural' or preferred roles;

- that an appointed leader (CEO, President, Chairperson, Captain, Team Leader ….) has a responsibility to encourage the contribution of members and even their leadership during relevant phases (in contrast to the oft-seen example of leaders who suppress others' contributions and try to 'own' everything themselves).

The 'group' referred to above could be a task group with 8 participants, a club with 50 members or a business with 1000 employees.

Our experience

Students are generally well able to understand that some people are ideas people, some are doers, some like to organise, some want to ensure everyone is getting along, etc. It is in this context that they realise that none of these roles is of higher status than another, even though we give them higher status names; e.g., chairperson, executive, etc.

Many students are also quite insightful in identifying their own and peers' natural roles, and even at seeing through a friends' public persona to their natural style.

Lesson 6 worksheet: GROUP ROLES — OBSERVATION SHEET

Look for some of these actions: Who …

Keeps people ON TASK?	CO
ALLOCATES JOBS to people?	
Sets PRIORITIES?	
Clarifies or SUMMARISES the discussion?	

Overcomes OBSTACLES?	SH
Influences how the group goes about its work?	
Shapes the DIRECTION of the discussion and the outcome?	
Pushes people to make a DECISION?	

Offers creative IDEAS?	PL
SOLVES PROBLEMS?	
Criticises ideas, but tries to promote BETTER IDEAS?	

Checks what OTHER GROUPS are doing?	RI
Gathers or offers facts and INFORMATION?	

QUESTIONS and challenges (helpfully) what is being said?	ME
ANALYSES problems, identifying all the options?	
JUDGES ideas?	

Turns the ideas into PRACTICAL steps?	IMP
IMPLEMENTS plans?	
Can't wait to do the HANDS-ON work?	

Keeps HARMONY?	TW
ENCOURAGES?	
Gets everyone INVOLVED?	
BUILDS on others' ideas?	

Watches the TIME (to get the job done, not because they want to go home)?	CF
Promotes a sense of URGENCY?	
CHECKS that everything has been done properly and there are no mistakes?	

Photocopiable page. Phil Ridden, *Lessons in Leadership,* www.philridden.biz, 2020

26

LESSON 7: UNDERSTANDING CONFLICT

Approximate time: 45 minutes

Outcomes

- Conflict is a normal consequence of people working together.

- How conflict is handled affects people's on-going work and relationships.

Learning experience

What is conflict?

Brainstorm synonyms for conflict. Then order these on a continuum from friendly conflict (e.g., debate, competition), through conflict which is destructive of property or relationships (e.g., aggressive protest), to dangerous and fatal conflict (e.g., war).

What causes conflict?

In groups, look at newspaper articles about conflict OR recount recent conflicts which students have experienced or seen. What caused it?

The answers might include

- wanting their own way

- wanting what someone else has

- not listening

- fear

- aggressive behaviour (which may provoke an aggressive response)

- limited resources (either personal, leading to theft, or national, leading to war)

- differing values

- injustice

- poor communication/misunderstandings

- self-interest (thoughtlessness, greed, selfishness)

- ego (protecting or enhancing one's self-image)

- prejudice and stereotyping

What escalates conflict? (Why do minor disagreements become major fights?)

Invite small groups of students to role play disputes which escalate. Review the drama to identify what caused the escalation. Answers might include:

- feelings (anger, frustration, impatience, quick to take offence)

- poor communication, not listening

- accusative language, blaming

- jumping to conclusions

- focusing on the person rather than the issue
- aggressive body language (posturing)
- win-lose actions

What defuses conflict?

Suggest ways in which the conflict shown in the role plays might have been defused. Answers might include:

- taking time out
- space (physical separation)
- non-accusative language (I statements)
- empathy (seeing the other person's viewpoint)
- assertive body language
- mediation …

Context

Adult courses in leadership and management often include a section titled 'Working with difficult people'. This is somewhat presumptuous, because whether a person is 'difficult' is not just a factor of their personality, but is also influenced by such things as the way others relate to them, the support and guidance of their supervisor (leader), and the situations they are required to deal with. Therefore, it is more helpful for students to understand that we each have our own way of being, relating and working, and the challenge for a leader is to enable each person in their group to 'bring out their best'. The previous lesson showed how we each respond to people and situations in a way which is inherent in our nature. This lesson and the next focus on ways to handle conflict so that it is productive, people grow and relationships are maintained or enhanced.

Conflict is normal, and not inherently wrong or 'bad'. Differing points of view, rigorous discussion, competitions, even protests, are all forms of conflict. However, how we respond to conflict may be morally wrong. Conflict becomes a problem when it leads to violence, property damage, and damaged relationships.

Conflict is handled well when each party feels that their opinion or wants or needs have been acknowledged and somehow accommodated (if not in full or not in their original form) and if the process maintains relationships between the parties.

The challenge is to manage conflict so that is does not become destructive, but enables people to learn and grow from the experience.

Our experience

Because of the intervention of adults in school and home conflicts, students may see all conflict as wrong. They may need help to see that conflict is not wrong; what is sometimes wrong is the way the conflict is handled.

LESSON 8 DEFUSING CONFLICT OR 'FIGHTING FAIR'

Approximate time: 45 minutes

Outcomes

- Conflict can often be defused by the use of appropriate strategies.
- Defusing conflict is a process of learning to 'fight fair'.

Learning experiences

Role play conflicts in which one person wants something from another person, but the other person is resistant.

It may be something tangible (e.g., a toy or electronic device), or something intangible (e.g., an admission or apology). You may choose to set up scenarios or allow students to create their own. e.g.,

- You want to have a turn on your friend's electronic game.
- You want your parent's approval to go to a party.
- You want your parent to run you to school because you're late.
- You want your teacher to revise your D for your assignment to a C.
- You want your sibling to admit that they cheated in a game.
- You want an apology from a peer for spreading a story about you.
- You are mediating between two younger students, one of whom is being bullied by the other.

Review the strategies used by people to get their way. Use *Lesson 8 worksheet: Assertiveness* to decide whether the strategies were passive, assertive or aggressive or even passive-aggressive.

Invite students to talk in triads about situations in which they have encountered each of these approaches, and to consider which approach they found most respectful and the most likely to maintain relationship.

Introduce the concept of 'fighting fair', the goal of resolving conflict without aggression or passivity, by using assertive strategies. However, people often resort to aggression in the 'heat of the moment', sometimes regretting this in retrospect. So discuss with students how they might become more skilled at using assertiveness rather than aggression when confronted with conflict. Refer to the previous lesson and actions which escalate or defuse conflict.

There may also be a need to discuss relationships with others (family, friends, peers) whose method is resolving conflict is passive or aggressive.

Context

Assertiveness is the most respectful approach to conflict resolution, and the approach which is most likely to maintain relationship. Yet, as indicated above, knowing is not the same as applying. Some people are easily 'wound up' by others; some fear aggressive confrontation so will yield; some are easily seduced by passive-aggressive strategies. Many students may cope daily with family or peers whose approach to conflict is unhelpful.

This may lead to sensitive personal issues for some students. This is a course on leadership, not counselling, so you may need to exercise judgement on when to terminate a discussion, and when to follow up a comment by a student at a later time.

In addition, your students may need further teaching on conflict resolution strategies such as mediation, negotiation and communication (including non-verbal communication), which are outside the focus of this course.

Our experience

As indicated above, many students (and adults) struggle knowing about these matters is not the same as applying them. We need to acknowledge that in the midst of a conflict situation it is not always easy to apply.

Lesson 8 worksheet: ASSERTIVENESS

Passive (weak) behaviour	Assertive behaviour	Aggressive behaviour
View yourself negatively, others positively	View yourself positively, others positively	View yourself positively, others negatively
Assume "I don't matter, you do"	Assume "I matter, you matter"	Assume "I matter, others don't"
Accept responsibility for others' feelings.	Accept responsibility for your own feelings	Make others responsible for your feelings.
Allow others to violate your rights	Claim your rights without violating others'	Violate others' rights.
Allow others to win while you lose	Look for solutions where both win.	Look for solutions where you win, others lose.
Freeze up with anxiety and lack of confidence	Ask confidently and without undue anxiety for yourself or others.	Intimidate others so that you make them anxious and destroy their confidence.
Suppress your feelings.	Express your feelings to others	Impose your feelings on others
Hope others will guess what you want.	Explain to people what you want.	Demand that others accept what you want.
Showing weak body language	Taking time to cool down	Shouting
Crying	Listening to others	Yelling
Being a doormat	Respecting others' rights, and your own	Verbal abuse
Hiding	Using friendly eye contact	Physical violence
Pretending conflict isn't happening	Having a calm, friendly expression on your face	Bullying
Letting other people push you around	Having a confident body posture	Harassment
Waiting for others to make the decisions	Respecting others' personal space when talking and listening	Wanting to dominate games
Going along with anything anyone says	Letting others express their feelings	Insisting on getting your own way
Not having any opinions	Stating your own opinions calmly	Mocking other people's opinions
Not standing up for your opinions	Taking responsibility for yourself	Using put-downs
Letting others solve your problems for you	Owning your opinions	Slamming doors
Letting others ignore you	"I" language	Sulking
Allowing others to invade your personal space	Allowing others to have their opinions	Manipulating people for your own ends
	Seeking solutions to conflicts	Refusing to talk about an issue
	Being strong, even taking charge, not to dominate others, but to get to a solution	Invading others' personal space
	Telling others when they infringe your rights	Accusing and blaming others
		"You" language
		Enlisting the support of other people.

Passive-aggressive behaviour: This is aggressive behaviour disguised as passive behaviour. Seemingly passive behaviours are used to manipulate others' emotions so that they yield. The insincerity of a passive-aggressive person is not always obvious, until it becomes a pattern of behaviour in which the seemingly passive person always seems to get their way, and yet the people around them are always left feeling guilty for not being more generous!

Photocopiable page. Phil Ridden, *Lessons in Leadership*, www.philridden.biz, 2020

CONCEPT 4: GROWTH — I AM READY!

The purpose of this section is to create in each individual an understanding that leaders do not have to be unfeeling and stoic. Leaders lead with the power of their personalities.

Understanding: By the end of the section, students may be considering, 'What have I learnt about leadership? How will I apply this new knowledge?'

Leadership attitude: We can continually improve our knowledge of leadership, so that we can say, 'I WILL BE READY TO LEAD WHEN NEEDED?'

LESSON 9: LEADERS HAVE FEELINGS TOO

Time required: Approximately 45 minutes

Outcomes

- Leaders have feelings too.

- My fears and other emotions are not a sign of failure, but give me the ability to understand others and myself.

- Self-doubt is a normal response, but not a crippling one.

- Leaders take risks, especially with their own image and comfort.

- Risks should be evaluated ethically to determine who is affected and how.

Learning experiences

Ask students to complete *Lesson 9 worksheet: Leaders have feelings too.*

Invite them to share responses in pairs/triads.

Explain that we each have different tolerances in our willingness to risk our physical safety, our image or reputation, and the affirmation of our peers. Yet sometimes people who lead must risk these things. Invite some students to share the circumstances which (they believe) would motivate them to go beyond their normal risk threshold.

Point out that all leaders must face the following issues from time to time:

- Will I make the wrong decision?

- Will I be blamed if we don't succeed?

- Will my leadership be challenged?

- Will I be able to defend the group's opinion or action?

- Will I have enough time, energy and knowledge?

- Will I crack under pressure and be embarrassed?

- Will this role enhance or damage my reputation and image?

In partner conversations, ask students to share when they have felt this way.

Ask whether they can think of other leaders who may have felt this way and when.

Share ideas on how to cope with these pressures.

Context

The purpose of the reflective activity is to help students consider their own levels of risk tolerance, and then to consider what circumstances would push them past those levels. Clearly, there is not guarantee that we will behave as we think we will in a situation. Throughout time, some people in particular circumstances have shown remarkable and inspirational courage beyond their imaginings, and others have fallen way short.

The second part of the lesson highlights that all leaders have self-doubt at some time. Putting forward an idea, arguing for a particular action, making a decision, and persuading others carry risks of damaged image or damaged self-esteem if things go wrong (and sometimes, even if they go right!).

A key to effective leadership is being prepared to take these risks. However, courageous leaders are not those who are careless with other people's lives, but those who, in the service of others, are prepared to risk their own reputation or safety.

Our experience

Students are reassured to learn that even leaders they admire have self-doubt and insecurities. It is not unusual to find that the principal who speaks so confidently at assemblies sometimes has panic attacks; that the political leader who presents confidently on the world stage leaves the podium to throw up with tension; that the drug-addled singer first took drugs to give him confidence to go on stage; that the

Lesson 9 worksheet: LEADERS HAVE FEELINGS TOO

If I think the answer in the book is wrong, I ….

When I think I see a better way of doing something, I …

When I'm faced with a new situation, I …

If I wrote a story I thought was better than books in the library, I would …

When people disagree with my ideas, I …

When I'm not sure how things are going to turn out, I …

When I have an idea, but I'm not sure what my classmates will think of it, I …

When I see someone being bullied or harassed, I …

If I found out that my friend has been bullying someone, I …

If my friends want to do something risky that I don't want to be part of, I …

If someone who needed my help, but my friends told me to keep out of it, I would …

If I believed in a cause, and my friends mocked it, I would …

If I could find the courage to risk it, I would like to …

I would be motivated to show unusual courage if …

When it comes to my physical safety, I like to be

☐ Very safe   ☐ Sensibly cautious   ☐ Somewhat reckless

When it comes to me image and reputation, I am usually

☐ Very careful   ☐ Reasonably sensitive   ☐ Dismissive

LESSON 10: MY LEADERSHIP

Time required: Approximately 45 minutes

Outcomes

- I can lead in some situations.

- I have some leadership qualities.

- There are some leadership skills or qualities I would like to develop further.

- Further development of my leadership skills is in my hands.

Learning experiences

Revisit the concept map from Lesson 1. Ask students to use this to assist them in completing *Lesson 10 worksheet: Reflecting on leadership.*

Invite students to share their self-assessment with a friend. The friend may be able to add insights which the student themselves overlooked, particularly in the area of strengths, as some students may tend to be self-effacing.

Present students with the following statement: *A leader is someone who leads when a leader is needed.* Then ask them to consider a time when they showed leadership, or when they could have showed leadership but didn't, and how they might have done things differently from the way they did.

Depending on the age of students, you might ask them to share, orally or in writing.

Context

Effective leaders are self-reflective. They reflect on situations before rushing into action (if time allows), and they are reflective about their own motivations and actions. It will assist students to grow as leaders if they can be reflective about their own leadership strengths and weaknesses, and what they learn from their experiences.

What have I learnt that stands out the most for me?	What are my leadership strengths?

What do I need to work on to be a better leader?	What would I like to know more about to be a better leader?

NOTES